Past Acquaintances

[Lost in time]

Love that is lost often times can't be rekindle because of the space in time. That old saying if you cast bread on the water if it returns back to you, it was meant to be, sometimes we are given a second chance, grab it and explore the love that is given back to you.

xulon PRESS

Class of 2012

Genie Simmons

Past Acquaintances

It was Lacey's 50th Anniversary and the department store was even more crowded with shoppers than usual. There were mothers with screaming kids and noisy teenagers loaded down with shopping bags, and it was only 10:30 in the morning. It was as if the people had waited outside all night, just to be the first ones in when the doors opened.

As a salesclerk at Lacey's, it was there that she met Michael Philip Morrison III. An attorney for Morrison, Haynes and Bryant, a well-known law firm here in Manhattan, he's been a customer for about five years at Lacey's. He had come in that morning with his mother Joanna; they separated as they entered. He was headed towards the jewelry department and she to ladies lingerie. He had come in to pick-up the diamond necklace and matching earrings that he had saw her eyeing a week ago. As he approached the clerk, he smiled and spoke.

"Good morning Laura, I'm here to get my favorite girl's birthday gift". "Good morning" Mr. Morrison, I have it right here ready for your inspection; she reached into the glass case and removed the necklace and earrings, he seemed quite please. He paid for his purchase, as he sign the card "Happy Birthday Mother, Love Michael." She wrapped the gift and handed it to him with the receipt.

It was at that moment that her supervisor and best friend Brandi walked up to her. "Laura", he said "you were selected as salesperson of the month, based upon sales, service and personality." She hadn't realized she had done so well. She smiled and accepted the roses, the gift certificate for Jon' Paul and the check for three hundred dollars. As tears cloud her vision in acceptance, she heard everyone clapping. Mixed into the crowd was Michael with a smile on his face. It wasn't hard to miss him being about 6ft 3in, olive completion with dark hair and green eyes. She watched as he left the store, and the customers disbursed and filtered back to their shopping.

"Brandii, I can't believe it, dinner at Jon' Paul's one of Manhattan's most exquisite restaurants. This is the first time since being here, that something as wonderful as this has happened to me". "It couldn't have happen to a nicer person, Laura, congratulations" Brandi said. With the roses in her hand, she looked at Brandii and smiled, "You know these are my favorite and to receive them from the store it's overwhelming. I can't remember the last time I got roses. Oh yeah, the last time I treated myself to them" she laughed. "So what are you going to wear to dinner, and when is the reservation for"? Brandii asked. "I have a week, to use the reservations, Laura said. "Will you watch my department? While I take these flowers to the break room and put them in water". It was on her way to the break room, that she spotted the little black dress on the clearance rack. She had Marsha, put it aside until her shift was over.

She went back to Brandii who was covering for her, she

thanked her. Time seemed to pass swiftly after lunch. Her last customer was a young lady in her late teens.

"May I help you," she asked.

She saw her eyeing the gold studded earrings in the case, and took them out.

"Yes, could I see those, please?"

As she took them out for her to get a better look at them, she commented on the fact that they were a hot item. "I've sold about five pairs of these today. It seems to be a trend with young people your age. They do look really nice on you, "said Laura. As Laura held up the mirror for her to look in, she smiled. "They do look nice don't they", was the young lady's response. "I'll take them", she said, and put them on my Visa"; as she put the last stud in her ear. "Thank you, and enjoy the rest of your evening", said Laura. "Bye," she said as she stop and turn around smiling pointing to her earring she was gone from sight.

It was 5:30 when Laura looked at her watch, it was closing time and she was glad. She paid for the dress that Marsha was holding for her. When she left the store it was 6:00pm. Her bus had just arrived, out of breath she had just made it in time; if she had been two minutes later she would have missed it.

It had been three days since she received the dinner reservation along with everything else. Thinking to herself if only she owed a car it would be so easy, NA-ah shaking her head not in New York the parking space would be costly. Calling ahead for a taxi and asking if he could be there at 7:20pm. She hung up the telephone and jumped into the shower. As she finished dressing, she slipped on the other shoe; it was then that she realized the horn blowing was that of the taxi. She grabbed her purse and locked the door of her apartment. As she got into the taxi, she could see he was a little annoyed; so she apologizes for making him wait. "Hey Miss", he said, looking through his rear view mirror, "you are one knock out; your date is one lucky guy". "Thanks", was her only response. "Where to lady" he asked. "Jon 'Paul's" was her only response. As she rode in silence, the taxi came to a screeching halt. "Twenty dollars Lady" he said. She takes a deep breath as she exits the taxi; as she was walking towards the entrance she heard the doorman as he opened the door. His complement was a "WOW! Some lucky guy he is." "Uh-huh" she grunted. "My name is Laura Simpson," she said "I have reservations for 8:30pm". "Yes, I see it here, would you like a window view or a corner table". "I'd like a window view, please". As he seated her at the table, he handed her a menu and said your waiter would be with her shortly. Looking around the restaurant Laura inhaled the aroma of the Lobster Bisque at the table next to her.

Laura was mesmerized by the décor; every table had a little candle with a top on it. The linen tablecloths and napkins were burgundy and white, folded in the shape of a bishop's crown. There was soft music playing in the background. It instrumental but she knew that melody, of course she thought to herself; My Cherie' Amore. She found herself humming to it, when she was tapped on the shoulder.

"Hello", the voice said. Turning her head to the sound of the voice she saw it was Mr. Morrison.

"I'm not interrupting am I"?

She smiled, "Nope just got caught up in the song".

"Have you ordered yet"? "I was pondering over the menu, can't seem to decide, everything looks enticing". I knew I should have taken French in high school instead of Spanish. Even in English it looks Greek".

"I think I can help, if I may". He took the menu from her hand, you'll enjoy Pommus deterre georgette, it's only potatoes stuffed with crayfish tails, served hot. For your first course, E'chalote, a small vegetable shallot and for your wine I suggest Beaujolais 1945. It was at that moment that the waiter came back and took her order. She thanked Michael for his suggestion and for ordering. It was at that moment that she thought to herself something about a man taking charge.

She couldn't help but smile, as she thought of her frequent dates; with them it was Kentucky Fried Chicken or some burger joint. They would never consider it, on their salaries.

But here she was Laura Lee Simpson at Jon' Paul's.

She ate her dinner in silence and watched the people on the veranda dancing to something by "Old Blue Eyes. It must have been a wedding party celebrating.

There was laughter and a lot of well wishes. The bride was beautiful, it was easy to see she was happy and in love. The groom was tall and handsome and was grinning from ear to ear, as he held his bride close. Laura was glad she decided to come this night, of enchantment and romance. It was then that she noticed that the other dinner guests were raising their glasses to the happy couple. Following the jester she did likewise. This would be a night she would remember.

The waiter had come back with her favorite cappuccino, French vanilla. She had sips a little when she noticed Michael with his mother. She thanked her for the warm birthday regards and hoped she enjoyed her dinner. Laura smiled, and told her she did very much. It was then that Michael said, he was sending his mother home with some of the family and asked if he could come back and join her for coffee and conversation. She smile and nodded at him; as she watched Michael escorted his mother to the family's limousine. At that moment the waiter had returned with a refill as Michael was pulling out his chair to be seated.

"I'll take my coffee black," Michael said.

"Did you see the wedding party that was out on the veranda," she said. "It wasn't hard to miss," he said.

She could feel Michael staring at her. The waiter came back and poured Michael's coffee, when he left the table Michael then spoke.

"You look exceptionally beautiful tonight". With her mind in a tailspin with questions, but dared not verbalize them, instead she smiled and said thank you.

She looked up from her coffee cup, to see this very handsome and charming man staring back at her.

"Tell me Laura, about yourself".

She begins to do something she had not done since kindergarten –stutter. "Really there isn't much to tell. She took a deep breath and started again. "As you know I work at

Lacey's, and I also attend Northern State University, Where I'm working, on my bachelor's degree in advertising and marketing. He sat there listening attentively to every word she was saying as he sipped his coffee.

"I come from a long line of singers. No one famous, my family is just small time and before your ask, NO, I don't sing." How did you know I as going to ask that anyway, "he said with a smile". "Let's just say you had that look, and I could see the wheels in your head turning." They begin to laugh at each other.

"Well I won't accept that since I heard you earlier humming 'My Cherie Amore,' "he said".

"Listen, when I do sing it's only in the shower," she said.

"I know what you mean. That's the only place I dare sing, but I think you are being a little too modest."

Laura felt herself blushing as Michael smiled at her.

"So finish telling me more, I am interested" as he signaled for the waiter to bring some more coffee. "Excuse me please; I would like to have a slice of cheesecake from the dessert tray". Michael cut in to say he'd like a slice as well. Before she could say another word the waiter was back with the cheesecake and coffee. "Thank you, "Michael, said as the waiter left our table.

"Well I tell you I left home when I was eighteen" It was then she couldn't help but laugh at herself.

"What's funny," he said.

"You know I couldn't help but remember how I was going out to conquer the big bad world." They both laughed. Not realizing how long they had been talking, the restaurant closed and everyone had left. Even the wedding party was gone. Time had passed so quickly; he was a good listener and very kind.

The waiter had covered up the piano and put the chairs on the top of the tables, neither one of them had realized just how late it was until one of the waiters walked over to them and informed them that they were closed. She felt utterly foolish for detaining him with such chattering, yet she felt like she was on a date. "Michael I'm sorry for detaining you so long."

"No! "He said, I've enjoyed the evening very much. "Well I suppose this is it; all good things must come to an end." He said as he pushed back her chair from the table and taking her hand.

"Thank you for an evening I shall never forget, and if I should ever need a lawyer, I'll remember you. Of course I hope that I never do."

"Hey, "he said with a smile.

As they walked out together they turned to each other at the same time; their eyes met. A thought came to her, a kiss would have been a conclusion to a perfect evening. They just stood there outside the restaurant looking at each other, when it started to rain.

"Good-night, "he said as he turned up the collar of his trench coat.

"Good-night Michael," She smiled at him as they waited on the attendant to bring his car around. Laura stood there in silence.

When the parking attendant came back with Michael's car,

he was about to leave when he heard the young man ask if she needed a taxi. "Yes, please,"

He whistled for one, the taxi pulled up to the curb, what had been a drizzle had now become a downpour. He barely missed drenching her with his taxi.

Michael came over after realizing Laura didn't own a car, apologized and said

"Thank you," and gave the taxi driver twenty dollars. "We won't need your services. Laura this gives us time to continue our conversation." It began to rain a little bit harder, Michael opened the door of his Jaguar and Laura got in as he closed the door. Michael ran to the other side got inside the car. She was soaking-wet. He turned up the heat on her side and then he reached over and pulled her seatbelt across her and fastened it.

"Now we are ready to go," he said.

Laura began to sneeze. He handed her a Kleenex, as she wiped her nose, she thanked him. "I'm sorry and please forgive me," she said.

"So where does the girl who's catching the cold live," he said, as he started up his car. "332 Lofton Street, apt B," she said through a sniffle. As he drove off, she could feel his eyes on her.

"I've enjoyed your company very much, Laura."

"Likewise Michael It's been a wonderful evening, despite the rain."

It was warm in the car; there was something soft playing on the radio. Laura felt her eyes getting heavy; it was difficult for her to keep them open. Her thoughts drifted, all she wanted to do was go home, soak in a hot bathtub and have a hot toddy. Laura didn't know she had been asleep, until she heard Michael calling her name.

"Laura, Laura, hey sweetheart wake up."

His voice was tender and loving; he then reached out and touched her hand.

"Oh, Michael, I am so sorry, I didn't mean to fall asleep on you. I felt so relaxed. You can blame it on the elements, the rain and the warmth of a cozy car." He smiled.

Feeling a little groggy, she put her hand over her mouth, to stop yawning. It was then that she noticed that it had stopped raining.

"I hope you aren't catching a cold," he said, handing her another Kleenex.

"I hope not, I think it's just these wet cloths that I'm in," she said. "Thanks again for the ride; I am truly sorry that you got wet on my behalf."

As she opened the car door she smiled at him and ran up the steps to her apartment building. She opened the door to the building and turned to see if he was still there. He waved and drove off.

Opening the door to her apartment, she turned on the lights and walked in. Tired and wet, she went to the bathroom and turned on the water in the bathtub pouring Calgon in the hot water. It was then that she realized she had not fed Elfie and Peddy their dinner. She came home early and in her haste she had forgotten to feed them. "I'm sorry, you guys," she said. The radio was on; otherwise the house was silent. She reached for the fish food and fed Elfie and Peddy, whom she considered her kids. She stepped into the tub that was warm and soothing; it felt good to her tired body. It was then that she heard Luther Van Dross' "Here and Now". She leaned back in the tub, smiled a warm smile as her mind went back to today's event.

The last thing she remembered was turning off the lights. The alarm clock woke her up at 7:30 in a startled jump. Feeling as though she had just gone to bed, she desperately wanted to stay in for another 10 minutes, but she knew that if she did the trouble she'd be in. She began to come alive as the hot water splashed her face and body.

She was dressed and eating a danish with her coffee, when she realized she had not called for a taxi. As she placed the call, her mind went back to last night. Michael and I, oh no what am I thinking. Reality check! It was a nice thought anyway smiling to herself; she glance at her watch, hoping the taxi would be there by the time she locked her apartment door. She remembered that the dispatcher said, one had just called in and said he was five blocks from Lofton Street. She closed the door of the building, turned around to see Michael outside leaning against his car.

"Michael, what are you doing here"! with a puzzled expression on her face.

"Good Morning," he said. "Yes it is", she said as she muffled the words from her lips. "What are you doing here?"

She was glad to see him and quiet surprised as well.

"You are as beautiful in the morning to, as you were last night"

As he stood there holding the car door open, he was grinning as though he was the cat that swallowed the canary.

"Madame your taxi await," he said. I didn't have any appointments this morning so I decided to drive you to work."

"Thank you but I have already called for a taxi."

"I know. He was here but I sent him away of course."

"Very funny, Michael"

"Well Lady will you get into this car or are you going to stand there and be late for work?" he said smiling".

"Ok," she said as they drove off.

"Why are you trying to be so difficult? You know I am a nice guy," he said as he reached out and gently touched her hand.

"I know Michael, and I think I can trust you," she said very mischievously with a smile.

As they drove in silence for what seemed like an eternity, Michael broke the silence. "Laura this is going to sound strange, but hear me out before you say anything. Evidently you don't know who I am."

"Yes I do," she said in haste. "I don't know any woman who is not familiar with the Morrison name. Sure there are a lot of Morrison's but not with your first name, Michael Philip Morrison of Morrison, Haynes and Bryant law firm. You and your family own hotels, motels, restaurants and a brokerage firm. You also own the Penthouse that you live in," she continued on, not even taking a moment to take a breath. "It was

22

at Westgate University that you earned your M.B.A. I was so impressed Magna Cum Laude! You are an achiever Mr. Morrison.

Michael you were educated at the best schools with a Ph.D. in law. I might have missed something. Oh! Wait a minute you were once engaged to some social lithe, a Miss Penelope Dupree. You see Michael, I do know who you are, surprised huh! Well if I missed anything forgive me. I haven't picked up a Buzz Magazine lately." It might be a rag magazine but sometimes it writes the truth.

It was then that she saw the disappointment in his eyes. As she caught her breath, he then responded.

"Are you finished now?" he said, sounding hurt and authoritative.

"Laura, now can I speak without any interruptions," he said.

"I'm sorry, Michael, please forgive my outburst, she said feeling very remorseful

"Please go ahead, I promise to remain quiet until you are finished."

"We met before I ever came into Lacey's five years ago. I didn't remember until

my mother told me. She was up late last night when I got home. There was something very familiar about you she said; she had seen you before Lacey's.

It really troubled her. Well she got out the photo album and started turning the pages. She remembered a little girl named Laura Elizabeth Taylor. When she was in the middle of the album there you were." Finding it hard to believe she kept her word and remain quiet.

"It was there that she found a black and white photo of you and me. It was taken in the back yard with you in the swing. You were 7 years old and I was 10 years old at that time. Your mother worked as our housekeeper, you could say we grew up together. Your mother would come on Tuesday's and she would always bring you with her. You were very shy and quiet; you would always sit in the kitchen while she polished

24

the silver. One day I asked you if you knew how to play chess, you didn't, so I taught you. You had these two long braids that looked like thick ropes that hung across your chest; you were skinny and had two front teeth missing. Well you did learn how to play chess; we spent that year doing different things. You had so much fun and so did I. We went horseback riding, ice skating you even loved to play cricket. We also went bike riding. We were the best of friends, you looked up to me and I took care of you. I was like a big brother to you. It was cute the way you would call my name Mickkey. Once I rode the bus home with Lea and you. She cooked some fried chicken, mashed potatoes and green beans. I remember that because the chicken was, what your mom said was smothered. "

He was smiling, as the memories became clear to him. Laura sat there trying patiently to keep quiet after all she had promise to until he was finished. The light had turned green as he continued down Third Street. Hoping not to get caught by another traffic light, she would be at Lacey's in five minutes.

"Two weeks had passed and you never came back. My mother was concerned, she knew something had to be wrong, so the next day my mother and I went to your house. I stood at the door knocking but there was no answer; a neighbor came up to the car, told my mother that two weeks ago your mother had died. We were shocked! The lady said the little girl was crying Mommy, Mommy hysterically. Bob who lived next door went in and found Laura Lea in the bed cold as ice. My mother asked about you. The lady said she didn't know. I couldn't believe it, you were gone and I didn't know where. Weeks had turned into months then years. There were times when I thought about that snag-a-tooth girl with those thick wavy braids. My mother knew how close I had gotten to you. It was some years later when my mother found out through Mary Alice the new house-keeper that you were in Kentucky with an Aunt Vergie."

As the car turned the corner she could see Lacey's and felt a sigh of relief.

It was as if he had her confused with someone else, maybe

26

he did she thought

to herself. "It was hard for the both of us, for we came to care very deeply about you and your mother. Even coming into Lacey's; I had no idea! It never occurred to me that you were the same Laura that I knew as a child. My mother wasn't even sure herself." He stopped the car in front of Lacey's Department store, where others had gathered waiting for the store to open.

"Michael I don't know what to say, except my name is Laura Lee Simpson".

"It's you Laura, alright he said."

"I'm sorry, and I do appreciate the ride but I have to go. They have just opened the door for me." As she opened the door to leave he grabbed her hand and looked at her with tender eyes.

"We will talk later. I promise," he said.

As Laura walked towards the open door, she didn't turn back to see if he was still there. She soon heard his car as he took off down Third Street. As she walked up to the door; she spoke to Brandi".

"Laura how was dinner at monsieur Jon' Paul's?"

"It was a night that I will always remember forever, she said,"

"Laura I can see it was good, so I will wait for the low down later after work."

"Brandi the food was fantastic, the scenery was that of class and the atmosphere was regal. I felt like I was in Paris, France. It was perfect. I will tell you more in detail later."

It was then that Brandi grabbed her by the arm and with a pushy attitude she began with the drill of today's event.

"Excuse me, huh right. I wasn't talking about the restaurant, I, like everybody else saw the car you got out of and who was that driving."

"I did say later after work. Ok? Do you think you can keep that over zealous imagination down a little?"

"Sure, Laura I will try," she said. "I will see you later Miss Salesperson of the Month," as she walked away laughing out loud.

Laura clocked in and began opening up her area. As she dusted off the jewelry cases, it was Michael that came to her thoughts; shaking her head to clear her thoughts. She found it hard to not think about him. Mondays are always slow and for some reason the day seemed to drag on. It was 10:30 and she had only sold three Rolex and one charm bracelet. She was in a mood, and couldn't shake it. 5:30 was not going to come any earlier just because she was in a stoop. She was ready to call it in, it was 12:25 but her replacement wouldn't be there to relieve her for five more minutes. Looking at the clock on the wall, time seemed to stop. It was at that moment that Joan appeared standing in front of Laura grinning. "I'm sorry, I'm late Laura. It's Jackie's fault. She was gossiping again, about somebody and a Jag." "Is that all she has to do is sit around and gossip? Hasn't she got any business of her own! Boy! some people."

Confused and puzzled at Laura's response, Joan could only stand there and apologize as Laura walked away. Yelling to the fact she would be in the lounge lying down, and tell that to Miss Jackie.

It was at that moment that she put her feet up on the sofa and laid her head down, and closed her eyes, when she heard someone calling her name. The voice seemed far away. "Laura are you in there? I'm coming in, are you all right?

She looked up to see Michael standing over her.

"Hello, I'm alright just a little tired."

"How long is your break, and can I sit with you for a while?"

"My break is for 30 minutes, and please sits. She patted the sofa for him to sit; she had to admit to herself, if not to him, she did find him attractive. Even though everything he had said to her earlier was so far-fetched. Thinking to herself everyone has a twin or a look-a-like some where in the world. And Michael had confused her with someone else.

Sitting down beside her, "Are you sure you're all right, or is something else going on." "Maybe a little too much wine; You know I'm not used to drinking wine older than I am," smiling at him.

"How did you know I was in here?"

"I heard you talking to the young woman, and she told me where to find you, there was this gleam in her eyes when I asked."

It was then that Laura busted out laughing.

"Forgive me," it's only then that she just realized who the gossip was about,

"Michael, why are you here?"

"Laura isn't it obvious? We have a lot to talk about. We do have some catching up to do don't you agree," as he pulled out the picture of them from his pocket.

She looked at the picture, it didn't register to her and she handed it back to him.

"I never imagine that a skinny, snag-a-tooth girl would grow up and become a beautiful woman and stubborn too. If you don't have any plans for dinner with anyone would you join me for dinner?"

"Huh! Thank you Michael, but I do have plans already with some friends at Eddies."

"Laura, there is something I need to tell you."

"I'm sorry but my break is over and I must get back to my department."

"Laura can't you get out of your plans? Please don't try to avoid me, smiling; it won't work you know."

"Michael I'm late."

"Laura, I'm not going to go away nor am I going to give up, count on that."

Opening the door for her he stepped in front of her and gently kissed her cheek. "You see I'm a very persistent person."

Later that day when it was time to close her department, she began to think about her aunt who had raised her. There were some bad and good memories growing up in her house. It wasn't easy for her to raise her six children and no man in the house. Then to get an extra child you didn't ask for.

Memories began to flood her thoughts, getting blamed for breaking a crystal vase that sat on the coffee table, for ripping her brand new summer dress. Her aunt once told her,

"I told your mama just because she was lighter than me, ain't no white man going to marry her; because she was pregnant and boy! Was I right? Didn't matter how pretty she was his family was never going to accept a mixed child. Either he left your mama or give up his inheritance and we all knew which he would choose." All my Aunt Vergie did was complained, Laura said to herself. I don't know why my mother died she was only forty-three; she was to young I remember wishing it had been my aunt instead. Her aunt's voice was clear in her head as she continued remember, "I don't know why your mama went and died on you, no insurance policy. I and your uncle had to bury her with our last little savings and with the help from the state. I hadn't seen her since she was fifteen, leaving her only child for me to take care of. A therapist would say, she had issues and they needed to be resolved.

"It's the past that I want to stay buried. Some things are best left that way," she said as she heard herself say it out loud." I promised myself as soon as I was old enough I was leaving. It was probably the reason Uncle Jackson left. He was a good man and one day he just never came home from work. She drove him away!"

I didn't think about them much, out of sight out of mind. I miss my mama; I spent many nights crying myself to sleep. My uncle I heard had died in a car crash some years later. I made up my mind as soon as I turned eighteen I was leaving

It was then that her friend, Brandi called out to her.

"Laura let's go."

"I'm ready, and I tell you I'm not kidding either."

"Well I can't wait to hear all about your day and not what Jackie had to say either. Her so called facts are never right, you know what I mean".

"You have no idea, Brandi."

"Oh you better believe I do, we all heard it from the shoe department, all the way down to inventory," laughing. "Everybody was talking about Mr. Michael P. Morrison. I like your spirit girlfriend; you are the salesgirl of the month!"

"Quit clowning and be serious, OK! You know I will tell

you everything all the glory details as you say. I'm in need of a serious unwind, and Eddies the place to do it." As they exit the store walking towards Eddies they could see Simon standing outside waiting. "It's a full house tonight so we have to squeeze somewhere probably at the bar. Gee Laura, I love you and all but you look like a train ran over you." Simon was sweet and he could really read me like a book, there was no hiding anything from him; just one of those long days."

"Right, Here's an opening in the back."

As they all sat down at the bar, they began to laugh.

"Now tell me somebody why are we laughing?"

"Oh! Simon, I really don't know where to begin. I'll try from the beginning."

"Laura! Does any of this have anything to do with the car you stepped out of this morning?"

"Uh-hum, it does I suppose".

"You know it does. Simon it was Mr. M.P.M himself," Brandi said smiling. "Go Laura, I've been waiting all day to hear this, and please don't miss a beat either."

The Barkeep knowing the three of them and there usual order, brought them their drinks, Simon a whiskey sour and Laura and Brandii had a red wine. It was then as Simon reached in the bowl to eat some beer nuts that he said, I'm waiting."

"It started at Jon'Pauls, Michael came over to my table order dinner for me in French. Afterwards we sat and had coffee, cheesecake and conversation."

"I like this girlfriend. You are like moving on up, a date with Mr. Money bags himself."

"It wasn't like that, Brandi. I thought he was being very nice, he was there when I was presented with the roses, the check and the reservation for dinner. He's also been a customer at Lacey's for many years."

"Ladies, please he is a good catch if I say so myself."

"One thing for sure Simon he is a good catch for any woman. He very wealthy and handsome, but he's a white guy, ok."

In unison Simon and Brandi said "what's color any way just a different pigmentation, we aren't living in the sixties."

"Gee are you guys' twins or something?"

Again they repeated themselves, "No!"

"Hey quit that," Brandi said to Simon turning to look at each other.

"Anyway, if you guys will let me finish, I will. This morning when I opened my apartment door he was there. Driving to work he told me, that my mother used to work for them as their housekeeper." Brandi gasped as in shock and Simon just sat there silent. "Yes, you heard me right. When he got home from the restaurant

his mother showed him a picture of me, which was taken in their backyard.

I told him, he had me confused with someone else. Actually it was his mother,

She said there was something about me that seemed to bother her. It was then that she found this photo. She remembered the deep dimples and the clef in my chin."

"Which you do have Laura."

"It could be anybody."

"I don't think so, Laura there are too many familiarities."

"Simon is right, Laura" Brandi said as she reached into the bowl for some more beer nuts". "Girlfriend I can count them, do you want me to?"

"He remembers me at seven years old, and it had been his mother who told him. You guys be real, Ok. He maybe just trying to reestablish a friendship, he thinks we once shared. I'm still not sure; I don't have any memory of it."

"Laura, you said he had a picture, right! Did you really get a good look at it?

"Well not really, I was on a break and he was just suddenly there."

"You see that's the difference in you and me if some knight in shining armor came to rescue me, you think I would second guess his motives; not Brandi Denise Washington. Uh hum."

"Hey guys! I already admitted I find him very attractive, I just think he is pursuing me only out of a long lost friendship. I will admit opposites do attract that's normal. It is just childhood memories ok. Did you know he taught me how to play chess, cricket and how to ride a horse, although I don't do any of these things now? I went to live with my aunt until I was eighteen, I got a partial scholarship from Northern State University and I never went back to Kentucky or to my aunt. "Wild! Girlfriend it must have been a trip growing up."

"That doesn't matter now Laura, Simon will be your protector," he said with a smile on his face.

"Michael told me that he and I were very close, I'm serious I don't have any memory of it. He said; I had come into his life at a crucial time; it was right after his father death. He really needed some one; it was hard on his mother as well. It was lung cancer. Michael was a loner; it was like having a little sister around the house. He said it made his mother happy to see us every Tuesday. Sometime when my mother didn't have to work, Mrs. Morrison would send the chauffeur to pick me up. My mother often served at the parties they would have and I came right behind her with my tray of petit fours".

"How cute, you must have been, Simon said", as he nudge Brandi on the elbow.

"I agree, such a darling little girl you were Laura, hearing the sarcasm in his voice"

"Ok! Keep this in mind this is Michael talking ok."

"Laura! why would Michael lie?" "That's what's wrong with you women you think all men lie, and that we all think with the other head. Please give a brother or a man the benefit of the doubt."

"Michael, heard the kids in my neighborhood teasing me about everything, calling me *'Lightly, whitely she's so brightly '* it would make me cry. Ignore them he said and then he would dry my tears."

"Sweetheart the man knows more about you than you do," Simon was holding my hand; then and grinning seriously.

"I've got to agree with Simon."

"It was Joanna, who put two and two together. She decided after coming into Lacey's that no two girls could look so much alike. After months of uncertainty she found the pictures she had been looking for. That night after dinner she showed them to Michael. He told me the dimples should have been a give away. But when you haven't seen someone in many, many years what could you expect."

"See what I mean, Laura, that's one ok."

"Yeah, Brandi I do see what you mean and number two the clef in the chin looks like or does it! Kirk Douglas."

"Please! Guys ease up on me, will ya. What was confusing to me was my last name on the back of the picture was Taylor.

"If your Uncle Jackson adopted you that would give you his last name, silly gir?."

"You know I have no documents or pictures. When I left

Kentucky I didn't turn around for nothing."

Brandi feeling very sentimental, "Oh this sounds like one of those fairy tales" with a happy ending in tow."

"Now you have heard the whole story about Michael and the girl he thinks I am, if there are any questions, too bad. Look I am tired and hungry, and besides it is getting even later as we sit. Can we please order?"

Opening up the menu in front of her, she signals for George the barkeep.

"Yeah, What will it be."

"First we will take that table in the corner, and then I want a steak medium with some fries with gravy on them and a beer," Simon said.

Brandi and Laura agreed on a Rueben sandwich with fries and a coke. As they left the bar for the corner table, Simon grabbed Laura's hand. And said "Girl it's not hard at all, when you start spending time with Michael everything that is buried in your subconscious mind will come forward and you will remember."

"Oh Simon you are such a wise man."

"Gee, Thanks Ladies."

"Laura what are you going to do?"

"Nothing; He didn't propose either did he ask me to move in with him, which I wouldn't. I said it once and I'll say it again all this attention is out of a past we once shared, only that."

"Look! Laura how do you know this for sure, maybe he is looking for something more," Simon said. "Have you looked in the mirror lately, you're a very attractive woman with personality, charm and charisma and a body that won't quit." It was at that moment that Brandi stepped on his toe.

"What am I chopped liver here?"

"Why Simon I didn't know you noticed." They laughed.

"It maybe that he is looking for a playmate too."

"Laura, I have to agree with Simon, my friend you are a very warm sensitive person and ok so you're beautiful."

Reaching over the table she gave her a hug.

"Laura it's easy for a man to be attracted to you even me," he said with a smile.

"There is an aura about you girl."

"You are going to make me blush ok, stop already."

"I don't think the color of your skin matters to him, nor where you came from which he knows already or who your third grade teacher was."

They finished dinner in silence.

Sipping her soda, the thought came to her, ask for advice and you will get it.

Brandi broke the silence once again. "I don't know about you, but I'm tired and ready to call it a night. How about you guys?"

"Yeah, I am too. Gee! I hadn't realized it was so late, where did the time go. It's 11:30 already." Simon asked for the check. Brandi and I were standing by the cashier as Simon paid our tab and dinner. "It's the middle of the week and you still have a hundred dollar bill. Ok that settles it we are doing this again, at your expense Simon."

"Sure ladies it's never a problem, I got to take care of my girls don't I," he said smiling. It was then that he grabbed Brandi and Laura around the neck. As they were walking out of Eddies' there was Michael, leaning up against his car with the door open.

"I thought you were going to be in there all night and I would have to go in there and get you."

"Michael this is Brandi and Simon." "Nice to meet you man. Come on Brandi and put those eyes back in your head, as he pulled on Brandii's arm dragging her to his car.

"Good night, I'll see you tomorrow. Bye," said Brandi smiling

"Get in! Laura, you have nothing to fear from me."

"I'm not afraid Michael not at all, what do you want from me or should I ask?"

Looking at him and the sincerity in his eyes almost made her want to melt into

his arms. Instead she just held on to the car door. As they

got into the car, he leaned over the seat and kissed her. "Laura I have been waiting to do this all day."

You know when you were young I loved you and wanted to take care of you and that has never changed, It explains a lot why I never married. It was fate that brought us together then and it's destiny that we should be together now. Why don't you give us a chance?"

"But, Michael!"

It was then that he kissed her again this time he smothers her lips as if to draw breath from her. Leaning into the kiss she felt it as he did. It was as if they both had quenched a desire so passionate that it was fire. There were no questions, no hesitation and no and turning back now. As they leaned up for air and looked into each other's eyes, she spoke, Michael do you like my answer?"

"Yes very much he said."

CPSIA information can be obtained at www.ICGtesting.com
Printed in the USA
BVOW03s2121041113

335451BV00002B/6/P